He comforts us in all our troubles
so that we can comfort others.

When they are troubled,
we will be able to give them the same comfort
God has given us.

II Corinthians1: 4 (NLT)

Helping Hurting Children:

A Journey of Healing

A Reference Guide for Caring Adults

(For Use in Conjunction with Children's Workbook)

Martha Faircloth Bush

WestBow Press books may be ordered through booksellers or by contacting:

WestBow Press
A Division of Thomas Nelson
1663 Liberty Drive
Bloomington, IN 47403
www.westbowpress.com
1-(866) 928-1240

Because of the dynamic nature of the Internet, any web addresses or links contained in this book may have changed since publication and may no longer be valid. The views expressed in this work are solely those of the author and do not necessarily reflect the views of the publisher, and the publisher hereby disclaims any responsibility for them.

Any people depicted in stock imagery provided by Thinkstock are models, and such images are being used for illustrative purposes only.

Certain stock imagery © Thinkstock.

ISBN: 978-1-4497-8524-6 (sc)

Library of Congress Control Number: 2013903291

Printed in the United States of America

WestBow Press rev. date: 2/18/2013

WESTBOW
PRESS
A DIVISION OF THOMAS NELSON

Contents

DEDICATION

This guide is dedicated to the memory of Melba Berkheimer and Dustin Brack.

Melba

The late Melba Berkheimer was my mentor and friend at Community Church in Orange, Texas, where she and her husband, David, were pastors for over thirty years. Melba's teaching on *The Grieving Process* helped many people discover healing after facing losses in life. She spent many years studying and researching this subject and passing on her knowledge to others. Her legacy lives on in the many lives she touched, myself included. Now, her work will continue as it touches the lives of children with principles from her teachings included in this guide. Without Melba's influence on my life, this book would not be a reality.

Dustin

Dustin's life was cut short at the young age of 11 in an accident, but not before he had made an impact on many people's lives. When Dustin met someone, his main objective was to find out if that person had a relationship with Jesus. He asked his music teacher before his first lesson if she knew Jesus. When she told him that she did know Jesus, he replied, "Okay, now we can begin."

The struggles Dustin's family had in coping with his death while still continuing to serve as children's church pastor at their local church, is briefly described on page thirteen in the endorsement written by his parents, Dan and Darla Brack.

ACKNOWLEDGEMENTS

Many thanks to...

My daughter, Heather, whose idea it was for me to venture into my first writing project. Her prodding, prompting, and encouraging words led me into one of the most exciting and fulfilling adventures of my life.

My husband, Glen, who worked many hours assisting me with his computer and document knowledge throughout the process of writing this book; I could not have done it without him.

My illustrator, Mel LeCompte, Jr. for his illustrations that I'm sure will capture the heart of every child reading this book. Mel has received two first place awards for his cartoon illustrations from the Louisiana Press Association. He is also the author and illustrator of two children's books: *The Ice Cream Cow*, and *T-Boy and the Terrible Turtle.*

Dr. Dianne Haneke, author and retired professor, who edited the first draft and who taught me much about my first plunge into writing from her years of teaching and writing.

My friends in Gloria Lee's Bible Study Group, Orange, Texas, who edited the second draft.

My daughter, Crystal, and sons-in-law, Tim and Hoit, who encouraged and cheered me along on my first writing adventure.

My mother, Faye, for her prayers.

All the professionals at Westbow Press who helped guide me through the publishing process of the workbook and reference guide.

And most of all I want to acknowledge and thank Jesus for healing this "little girl's broken heart" and giving me the desire to pass his message of healing onto other children.

ENDORSEMENTS

We lost our son, Dustin, at the age of 11 in an accident. Our two daughters, Lindsay and Haley, were left trying to make sense of a shattered home where life would never be the same. They experienced times at school, church, and with friends where they were just not understood and many times felt their pain went unheard.

This book is a life-saver for parents, grandparents, children's pastors, and teachers to have some understanding of how to help a child who has experienced loss. I believe this will be a valuable tool that will aid in the healing of many children who wake up one day and find their lives turned upside down by the loss of a loved one.

If you want to truly minister to the children who are hurting with grief, then you will definitely want to keep this workbook at your fingertips. As parents who have walked this path, this book is like bread and water to us as we try to help our children.

Reverend Dan and Mrs. Darla Brack

Children's Church Pastors, Community Church
Orange, Texas

Children suffer various losses during their childhood with little or no knowledge of how to cope with those losses. As children grieve differently than adults, the normal grieving responses may not be recognized; consequently, children are often left to deal with their grief alone. I am pleased to recommend this resource as an easy-to-use guide for those parents, grandparents, children's church leaders, or others who desire to help, but who may have felt powerless or unsure as to how to do so.

Virginia G. Johnson, Licensed Professional Counselor

Credentials: LBSW, LCDC, M.Ed. LPC

Martha has done an excellent job taking the most common steps in dealing with a loss and putting them in a very teachable format for children. As I read the manual, I knew it would be a great tool for anyone working with children.

As a children's pastor for several decades, I plan on applying these principles to help children work through losses in their lives. Whether you are a parent, a teacher, a mentor, or a counselor, you will truly be blessed by knowing and sharing these principles.

Rev. Lisa Ellermann

Founder of:
    Camp His Way Children Camp, Jasper, Texas
    Camp His Way Children Camp, Chennai, India

FOREWORD

I have known Martha Bush as her pastor for well over two decades. During that time she has studied, taught, and helped both adults and children to find their identity in Christ. She is writing from experience, deep study and much success in helping people to overcome past hurts, losses, abuses and rejections.

She knows the valuable treasure that lies in the hearts of God's kids and seeks to release it. So many see the future as hopeless and themselves as worthless due to ill treatment and circumstances. Their whole interpretation of life is skewed so that everything they do fails before they get started, thinking that they are worthless without value to both God and man.

Can abused and hurting children be reached with this message? If they are capable of learning several languages at the same time before the age of six as well as thinking in those languages, surely God's loving Word and the compassion of living human beings can reach them deep inside. Besides knowledge, Martha knows that the presence and love of God can easily be experienced and felt in their lives.

I know Martha Bush. I've seen her efforts, work of love, and successes. I know the principles and the God she serves works miracles in the lives of adults and children. So, I wholeheartedly recommend her writings.

David Berkheimer

Former pastor of Community Church (32 plus years)
Orange, Texas

Introduction

Dear Caring Adult:

Welcome! I'm so glad you are joining us on our ***Journey of Healing***. I promise you it will be one of the most valuable and rewarding experiences you have ever undertaken as you become an instrument in God's hands in ***Helping Hurting Children*** heal from losses in their lives.

A loss is a separation from someone or something of value to us. Our children today are faced with many issues resulting in losses. Some of the issues facing them are:

- **Death**
- **Divorce**
- **Abuse**

- **Multiple Moves**
- **Family Addictions**
- **Parental Imprisonment**

- **Terrorism**
- **School Violence**
- **Natural Disasters**

For the most part, we know very little about losses or what to do with them when they occur. Children, in particular, are often over-looked during a time of loss and the pain that accompanies it. Why?

1. Sometimes adults, unintentionally, get caught up in their own pain and they fail to recognize that their child is also hurting.

2. Often times, a child's pain is overlooked because children do not express their pain in ways adults recognize.

3. **Probably the #1 reason children are overlooked during times of loss is because the primary adult in the child's life just simply doesn't know how to help the child.**(1)

While there can be no concrete or cookie-cut answers in dealing with losses, children need guidelines to help them cope with the hurt associated with it. ***Helping Hurting Children: A Journey of Healing*** is a workbook for children written specifically for that purpose. It is designed to lay a solid biblical foundation in the early years of a child's life to help him meet with losses that occur on a daily basis. It also serves as a hands-on tool that parents, grandparents, children's ministers, school officials, lay counselors, or any caring adult can use in implementing the fundamental principles needed in helping a child find healing from the emotional scars of losses.

This accompanying Reference Guide you are reading is written with the intent to enlighten you, the caring adult traveling with him, to a child's emotional state of mind during a time of loss in his life. Prayerfully, it will keep you from being "caught completely unaware," as you help him process his grief and answer the questions he might have.

Certainly, I am aware of the fact that many children may need the help of a professional counselor to address problems beyond the scope of the children's workbook and Reference Guide. May we all work together to become the catalyst in helping a child grow into adulthood free of hurts from his childhood.

Let me introduce you to the chapters in each book, starting with the children's workbook. The reading level and the activities are appropriate for children ages 7 through 12, but can be adapted for older or younger children as well. I recommend you familiarize yourself with both the children's workbook and Reference Guide prior to beginning your journey with the children.

Children's Workbook

Loss and Grieve Defined: The first 4 chapters set the stage by defining the word *loss,* along with facts and examples of losses, and also by defining the word *grieve.* Most grief counselors would agree that grieving involves certain stages, such as denial, anger, bargaining, acceptance, but not in any particular order. Keeping those stages in mind, I have chosen to expand on the following topics for this workbook. I believe they will be beneficial for children to learn to apply at an early age when grieving the emotional stress of a loss.

1. **Recognizing Feelings**
2. **Expressing Feelings**
3. **Forgiving Others**
4. **Asking Others to Forgive You**
5. **Accepting a Loss**

Bible Story: The concept taught in each chapter is followed by a Bible story. Such familiar characters as Joseph, David, Cain, and Abel help make the concept of each teaching come alive through stories from their own lives.

Activities: The Bible story is followed by activities for the child to work through that are designed to help break down those walls children sometimes put up after a loss. It is through these activities the child is invited to express his grief in such ways as: talking, writing, drawing, dancing, or play-acting. In essence, the activities provide for him his "own special place" where he can go and be himself. Also included in these activities are tips to help build up a child's self-esteem which sometimes spirals downward during a loss. Bubby the Rabbit, introduced to the children in chapter 1, shares tips and scriptures from the Bible to accomplish this feat. Much emphasis is also placed on scripture memorization and prayer.

Journey Friends: As an added feature, five children travel this ***Journey of Healing*** with the children with whom you are working. They tell their true story of a loss they have experienced, their journey through each of the steps associated with grieving, and their efforts to move forward. These journey friends will help the child you are traveling with have a connection with kids their own age who have experienced losses in their life.

Suggestions for Teaching

1. **One on One --** Depending upon the type of loss, a child may need individual attention. If so, carefully guide him through each chapter, keeping in mind the importance of not rushing him, but allowing him time to absorb each step.

2. **Groups --** Any one of the chapters can be utilized in group studies. Each topic is crucial for building a spiritual foundation in dealing with life on a daily basis. This foundation will go with him into adulthood, equipping him to face the storms of life. Be creative when teaching in groups. Involve the kids in dramas or puppet shows to make the concepts and Bible story come alive.

3. **Personal Growth** -- Along with walking the child through the grieving topics as outlined on the previous page, three additional points should be gently implanted into the child's life along his journey.

(1) Lead Him into a Personal Relationship with Jesus Christ

In chapter 7, the child is given an opportunity to receive Jesus; however, always be on the alert to the Holy Spirit's prompting at any time during his journey.

(2) Teach Him the Value of Giving Thanks

As adults, we often look only on the dark side of life when we encounter losses in our life, and forget to count our blessings. Grab hold of every opportunity to teach the child with whom you are working to give thanks. This helps move him forward in the healing process.

(3) Teach Him the Value of Helping Others

As you probably know already, one of the greatest joys in life comes when we help others. Why not instill this in a child at an early age, even in the midst of any loss he might have experienced. Watch him move forward in his own healing process, as he gains a sense of joy when he begins to help others.

❋ ❋ ❋ ❋ ❋ ❋ ❋ ❋ ❋ ❋ ❋ ❋

Reference Guide

Chapter 1: Supporting a Grieving Child

Often what adults label as "bad behavior" in children is a cry for help after experiencing a loss. This chapter offers basic tips in recognizing the signs of grief in children.

Chapter 2: Understanding Emotions

Emotions are the <u>bulk</u> of the grieving process. Your understanding of the emotions a child exhibits can pave the way for him to be able to express his emotions in a healthy way in the midst of losses in everyday life.

Chapter 3: Recognizing Perception

Children perceive and view things that happen to them in their childhood with childlike wisdom, childlike knowledge, and childlike understanding. Because of this, a child often perceives a loss entirely wrong, thus causing him more pain. This chapter is to help adults guard against wrong perceptions during and after a loss has occurred.

Chapter 4: Building Self-Esteem

During a loss, a child's self-esteem may begin to spiral downward. Our mission as caring adults is to help build self-esteem in children based on how much God loves and values him in order to become all that God created him to be. Bubby the Rabbit will assist you in this endeavor by giving the children tips, scriptures, and questions to answer in the activities section of each chapter.

Chapter 5: Answering Questions about Specific Losses

When a child experiences a loss or knows of someone who has, questions arise out of his struggle to understand the concept of what is happening. This chapter lists questions children might ask concerning: **Death, Bullying, Moving, Loss of a Pet,** and **Divorce.** Answers have been provided for you to use as a guide to meet the child's curiosity.

❋ ❋ ❋ ❋ ❋ ❋ ❋ ❋ ❋ ❋ ❋

Why I Decided to Write This Book

My introduction to hurts and losses and how to grieve through them came from the late Melba Berkheimer, who co-pastored with her husband, David, at Community Church, Orange, Texas. She approached me one Sunday morning at church and handed me a 45 minute cassette tape of one of the many times she had spoken to groups on the subject of grieving. Our conversation went something like this:

"I'd like for you to teach adult classes on The Grieving Process at church for the next three months." As a former school teacher, I was accustomed to having a teacher's manual at my disposal, so I asked: "Do you have a teacher's manual?" "I have no manual; all you need is this tape," Melba replied.

And so it was, my first class began with just "me and the tape." That three-month class turned into a ten-year journey of meeting weekly with hurting adults. Along the way, I spent hours researching losses and how to grieve through them. I gleaned much from the writings of many Christian psychologists on grieving, as well as learning more about the overall emotional, relational, and spiritual development of people in general. I am indebted to their wisdom, which has set forth the principles and insights for the children's workbook as well as the Reference Guide.

Throughout the years of teaching adults, I began to see a pattern emerge from women and men who came into the class to grieve through a current loss. I witnessed them come to the realization that, not only did they need healing from a current loss, but they also realized some of their childhood hurts had not been resolved from long years ago.

With that discovery, I began to see the importance of building a foundation for children at an early stage in life to help them cope with losses. This was confirmed to me the night that Dan Brack, the children's minister at my church, approached me with these words: "Can you help me? I've got some hurting children in my services."

As I began researching grief in children in an effort to write a study course for Dan, I came across a book, entitled ***Recovering from Losses in Life***, by H. Norman Wright. One simple sentence in that book set the wheels of my passion for helping hurting children on fire. Mr. Wright stated:

"Probably the #1 reason children are overlooked during times of loss
is because the primary adult in the child's life
just simply doesn't know *"how to help the child."*

And so, with encouragement from my daughter, Heather, my passion for children expanded beyond the walls of my local church. I became determined to put into the hands of parents, grandparents, children's ministers, school officials, lay counselors, and any caring adult a hands-on tool to implement the fundamental principles needed in helping a child find healing from the emotional scars of losses.

Thus, ***Helping Hurting Children: A Journey of Healing*** was birthed.

Have You Faced Your Own Hurt?

As you work through this process of emotional healing with a child, don't be surprised if memories of losses from your own childhood begin to surface. If so, ask yourself: "Have I grieved over these losses or not? What grieving work do I need to complete?"

Also, if you are a parent or grandparent guiding a child through healing after a loss, you might be experiencing the same loss, such as the death of a family member or a divorce. Though written on an elementary level, the topics most commonly associated with grieving are the same for adults as they are for children in order to heal the hurt.

As the author of this guide, it is my prayer that by ***Helping Hurting Children,*** you, too, may experience a healing in your own life. May God bless you and the children as you embark on a ***Journey of Healing***.

Martha Bush

Chapter 1

Supporting a Grieving Child

Quoting from Linda Goldman, professional grief therapist and counselor:

"The adult world often judges and labels children negatively for their behaviors. Many of our children are often labeled ADD or ADHD, "slow learners" or troublemakers ----- and when they spiral down far enough, they are then criminalized, hospitalized, or buried."[1]

Linda goes on to say that this is happening because the adult world does not recognize the signs of grief in a child. If we did, then we could help them before their pleas turn into screams and before the screams are forever silenced.

With that thought in mind, the purpose of this chapter is to offer a few basic tips to help you recognize the signs of grief in the life of a child, as well as ways to support him during his grief.

1. Common Signs of Grief

One of the best ways to recognize that a child is in grief is a change in his behavior. It is important for parents, educators, or any adult associated with the child to share with one another noticeable changes in behavior. This could be a strong force in differentiating between grief and ADD or LD.

Normal changes in behavior due to grief might include:[2]

- not eating well
- trouble sleeping or having nightmares
- bed-wetting
- become withdrawn and unsociable
- not completing schoolwork
- problems listening and concentrating on school work
- bursts of anger in the form of hitting and punching others
- difficulty in following directions
- acting out as the class clown to draw attention to himself
- stop participating in activities he normally enjoys

2. Everyone Grieves Differently

It is important to realize that everyone grieves differently due to many influences in their life. Religious beliefs, cultural traditions, family experiences, and personality differences all play a part in the way a person chooses to handle his grief, including children. You might say each child has a different and unique experience all of his own when he is in grief.

3. Be Aware of Physical Signs of Grief

It is true that grief sometimes brings with it stomach aches, headaches, or other tension related symptoms in the child's body. However, if these physical pains persist, it is best to have them checked out by a doctor rather than assuming it is all grief related.

4. Grief Comes in Waves

How often have you heard yourself or another adult say: "I thought I was doing okay, and then it was like a big wave hit me." Children are no different. Sharon, a young volunteer at a grief center, described her grieving a childhood loss as a series of waves; some of which were big and stormy, and others calm.(3) While children may return to a somewhat normal lifestyle, all of a sudden another wave of grief might descend upon them. This does not mean that they are regressing. It might mean that he suddenly had a memory of happier times prior to his loss, and a wave of grief washes over him for someone or something he lost that was of value to him.

5. Healing is a Process

Dr. Phil McGuire once said: "Time does not heal; it is what we do with time that heals." Our mission as caring adults is to guide and help children know what to do in the time period he has experienced a loss. Be patient and do not rush him through the process.

6. Listen

Restrain from giving advice, offering up opinions, and above all passing judgment when the child wants to tell the story of his loss and the feelings he might have. As he sees that you are not passing judgment on him for what he says or how he feels, a trust relationship is built, which he desperately needs. When he is silent and not talking, listen to that message as well. In short, pay attention to what is being said, as well as what is not being said.

7. A Child is Limited in How He Expresses Himself Verbally

Because of his verbal limitations, he often expresses his grief in actions which are not consistent with his age, as well as his normal behavior. You might see him exhibit unusual anger or silence. Remember also that some children are naturally quiet and not verbal; however, once they feel you can be trusted, they often open up and talk more. Don't push, wait patiently.

8. Do not Try to "Fix" a Child's Hurt

Adults have a tendency to want to **"fix" or "soothe" over a child's hurt**, rather than allowing him to go through the pain. Children don't need to be fixed; grief is a normal and healthy response to loss. Allow them to grieve.

9. Caution

Children often respond the way they think adults want them to respond, therefore asking questions that require a "Yes" or "No" answer should be avoided. Prodding a child for answers should also be avoided.

10. Different Ages - - Different Responses

Understanding what a normal response is for a child in a particular age group is a tremendous advantage to understanding how a child processes his grief. In his book, **_It's Okay to Cry_**, H. Norman Wright, gives the thinking process of children in ages 5-12.

- **Ages 5-8**: Under the age of 5, it is sometimes difficult for a child to understand that losses are permanent. By the age of 5, they may realize the loss is permanent, but cannot connect to it emotionally, nor do they know how to respond to it.(4)

- **Ages 9-12**: Children in this age bracket are developing changes in their thinking process. They are beginning to understand the meaning of loss, as well as some of the changes that will take place as a result of the loss. However, because their thinking is still not fully developed, conclusions could be reached that are not accurate.(5) Communicate closely with him to help him see the "bigger picture" of his loss clearly. [See Chapter 3 in Reference Guide: Recognizing Perception]

11. Playing is Grieving

Do not be surprised if right in the middle of a conversation with the child about his loss that he wants to go outside and play. Allow him to do so. Playing can be therapeutic for him, and bring a moment of joy into his young life in the midst of a trying situation.

12. Be Sensitive to Holidays

Adults can relate to the statement that "the holidays are much harder to face following a loss." This is also true with children. Extra effort should be put forth to help the child celebrate holidays, such as birthdays, anniversaries, Christmas, etc.

13. Faith During Grief

When life throws weighty issues at young children, their view of God can become distorted. "If God is so good, why did my daddy die, or why didn't God keep my parents from divorcing," he might reason. Let's face it -- adults play this same scenario out in their own minds during a time of crisis. You might say a child could become **unbalanced** in regard to how he once viewed God when he goes through a loss. During this time, the caring adult should try to help the child **balance his grief and faith in God.**

14. Family Grief

If you are a parent working through grief with your child, it is very possible that you have experienced a loss at the same time as your child. This happens particularly in times of death and divorce. It is okay to tell your children you are sad. As a matter of fact, it probably will help them realize that it is okay to share their own feelings.

15. Counseling

This book is designed to give all caring adults a tool to use in helping children through losses. However, some children may need the help of a professional counselor. If you feel this is needed, contact the child's school counselor, doctor, minister, or local hotline to assist you in helping the child.

Chapter 2

Understanding Feelings

Feelings, or emotions as they are also called, are defined as our responses to events that happen in life. Learning to express their feelings, while at the same time having good behavior, is vital for a child's overall emotional health. Adults are the key to helping him obtain balance.

In chapters 5 and 6 of the children's workbook, you will find several exercises devoted to helping children Recognize Feelings and Express Feelings. Do not rush through these chapters; it is here that children learn lessons of a lifetime. Often times, a child is never given the opportunity to express his feelings during childhood. As a result, it cripples him as an adult in making wise decisions because he has never been given the freedom to express himself.

As you will see in chapter 6, the children are asked to pour out their feelings about their loss using several blank pages that are provided. These pages can be treated as a journal, whereby the child comes back to them time and time again to "keep on pouring" when a wave of grief hits him. Carefully observe the child and encourage him to pour out his feelings in healthy ways, as noted in this chapter. Also, help him decide which ways are best suited for him.

The following are pointers for you to keep in mind when dealing with his feelings.

1. Validate All Emotions

Often adults may be shocked by what children say as an expression of their feelings. Refrain from saying, "You shouldn't feel that way," but, instead allow him a safe environment in which to express all of his feelings without fear of being put down. It would be safe to say, "You must stay *'shock-proof'* at anything the child might say."

While validating his emotions is a must, correcting wrong behavior is also a must. There is a big difference between "Okay Feelings" and validating those feelings verses allowing "Wrong Behavior" that could be harmful to him as well as others to continue.

2. True and False Guilt

Children often feel that losses are their fault and have deep feelings of guilt. This is especially true with death and divorce. It is normal to hear a child make statements such as: "If I had prayed more for my loved one, he wouldn't have died." "If I had been a better kid, my parents would not have divorced." "It must be my fault."

Children must be taught that there is a big difference between true guilt and false guilt.

- **TRUE GUILT:** True guilt is **wrong behavior,** which comes from the conscience when having done something wrong.(1) Having this feeling is a **good thing**, because it is a time to look at behavior that needs to be changed such as: punching, fighting, or hurting others. Take this opportunity to encourage him to ask Jesus to forgive him of wrong behavior, apologize to the person he hurt, and show him ways to make a turn-around in his behavior.

- **FALSE GUILT:** False guilt is when **nothing** has been done to cause a particular thing to happen, such as a parent's divorce or the death of a family member.(2) Try this simple exercise with him to help him see the difference. Have the child make a list of all the things that are causing him to have guilty feelings. Go through the list with him, pointing out the ones which are false. Then have him throw the false guilt list in the garbage can.

3. Good Anger - - Good Fear - - Good Worry

Recognizing and Expressing Feelings, as taught in chapters 5 and 6 in the children's workbook, is a must to teach children at an early age in order for them to learn "how to get in touch" with their feelings and at the same time have "good behavior." However, they also need to know that there are times when it is **good** to have anger, fear, and worry as a positive emotion. For example:

- **GOOD ANGER:** An example of good anger might include seeing another child being bullied. Their anger would allow them to go with the child to tell an adult rather than letting the bullying continue.

- **GOOD FEAR:** Good fear helps a child to have a healthy sense of caution, such as fear of strange dogs and strange people, which can be dangerous for them.

- **GOOD WORRY:** Good worry might include his grades in school. It is good to have a certain sense of worry or at least a deep feeling of concern in order to improve on study habits that will help keep his grades up to par.

4. Checklist For Signs of Depression(3)

It is natural for children to have feelings of sadness after a loss. If sadness is prolonged, it could mean a sign of depression, which should be treated by a professional. The National Mental Health Association gives a checklist to assess depression signs.

Feelings	Physical Problems
guilt	headaches
emptiness	stomachaches
hopelessness	lack of energy
worthlessness	has problems sleeping
does not enjoy everyday pleasures	changes in weight or appetite

Thinking Problems	Behavioral Problems
has hard time concentrating	not wanting to go to school
hard time keeping up his grades	desires to be alone most of the time
slow in completing school work	drops out of sports/hobbies, activities
has hard time making decisions	restless

5. Be Aware of the Silent Voice of Pain

Make it a point every day to ask children questions about their life in general as a means of encouraging expression of feelings, less they become silent during a loss.

- **Bottled up Emotions:** Without guidance, children do not know what to do with the emotions they are having during a crisis situation in their life. Some keep their emotions bottled up inside of them out of loyalty to the adult in their life. They sometimes feel that expressing their emotions only brings more heartache to their parent. I fell into that category as a child. As for my own two children, it was easy for one daughter to express her emotions. However, the other daughter was a joyful, free-spirited child who was void of much personal conversation. I overlooked her care-free spirit as being "emotionally okay" only to learn in later years, she had kept her emotions bottled up on various issues.

- **Physical Display:** While the silent child keeps his pain all bottled up inside, other children may be expressing their pain, but often in an unhealthy way. The story of Katy is a prime example. Her parents were getting a divorce. Her older brother discovered that Katy was cutting herself with a razor blade all up and down her arms. She began wearing long sleeves in the summertime to cover up the marks. When confronted with the long sleeves, she downplayed her actions by saying she was making a fashion statement of her own.

6. Preventing Negative Emotions From Becoming Patterns

When a negative emotion such as anger, fear, depression, or false guilt is repeated over and over again, it can become a pattern or a normal way of responding. That pattern can become destructive to the child, as well as others. When negative emotions are not dealt with in childhood and brought under control, they usually become the way he responds as an adult. He may accept adult responsibilities, but still be responding in the negative pattern that was established in childhood.

7. Different Temperaments

Studies show that there are 4 basic temperaments that describe everyone's personality. Each of these temperaments carries with it a particular emotional response to life's circumstances. Further teaching on this subject would help you understand the temperament and responses of children. Check with Amazon. com or your local book store for books dealing with this subject.

8. Build a Foundation Based on Prayer, Scripture Memorization, Exercise

This "three in one step" was listed as one of the **Okay Ways** of Expressing Feelings in chapter 6 in the children's workbook in order to have good behavior. Learning to use this step in childhood will, not only help him control his emotions as he copes with losses as a child, but will also enable him to lay a solid foundation for controlling his emotions as he enters adulthood when losses continue to filter into his life.

Therefore, avail yourself to every opportunity to:

(1) Encourage him to <u>PRAY</u> when he feels emotional distraught. Stress to him the importance of praying and asking God to help him keep his emotions in control when he is faced with situations in his life. Also, pray with him and encourage him to ask others to pray for him to help him through emotional times in his life.

(2) Encourage him to <u>MEMORIZE SCRIPTURES</u> that pertains to a specific emotion he is trying to control, such as anger or fear. Suggest that he write those scriptures in his workbook and review them with him often.

(3) Assist him in developing a consistent <u>EXERCISE PROGRAM</u>. The Bible says in 1 Corinthians 6:19: "Haven't you yet learned that your body is the home of the Holy Spirit God gave you, and that He lives within you" [TLB] Teach children that God gave us our body, and we are to keep it healthy through proper food and exercise. In addition to keeping the body healthy, exercise is also a way of relieving the stress children might be experiencing because of a loss.

9. Modeling Balanced Emotions Before Children

An adult modeling balanced emotions before children is one of the best teaching tools a child can have in regards to learning how to control his own emotions. However, for an adult to model healthy emotional responses before a child comes with two clarifications:

(1) Adults should not try to hide their emotions from a child by pretending that everything is "okay" after a loss in their own life. Children need to witness the adults in his life displaying emotions. Its best they realize at an early age that not everything is going to be a "winning" situation. Every little detail about the loss shouldn't be told to the child; however, he needs to know that adults have hurts and losses also.

(2) On the other hand, adults have an opportunity to be a role model to children by expressing their emotions in ways in which they are in control of their behavior and actions. Certainly erratic behavior in the form of yelling, screaming, cursing, etc. means they are not in control of their emotions.

Chapter 3

Recognizing Perception

Have you ever tried to drive with a dirty windshield? Obviously your view would be distorted, thus running the risk of an accident. Because we see only part of the picture we call life, this is the same dilemma we face as we try to cope with life based on our limited perceptions. Sometimes we get it right, sometimes we don't.

Perception is defined as the mental grasp of objects through the senses, insight, how we view things.(1) Children's perception during or after a loss can be very distorted, mainly because they are viewing and analyzing things with childlike wisdom, childlike knowledge, and childlike understanding. Therefore, the real truth of a loss may be erroneous. Some examples of wrong perception are:

1. **My Fault Syndrome**

   Probably #1 on the list of distorted perceptions is when a child believes losses are his fault. Children often believe that if they had been a better kid, their parents would not have divorced. Some even perceive death as their fault by thinking "if I had only prayed more, my loved one would not have died."

2. **Interpretation of marital problems of parents**

   Kids who see Mom and Dad fighting may assume they know the reason for the fight when, in essence, it could be their interpretation of the problem. The real reasons a couple is having problems are <u>bigger</u> than kids can understand. They cannot see into the world of grown-ups and all that it involves.

3. **Parents Who Never Allow Children to Know About Their Disagreements**

   Let's face it -- there are no Norman Rockwell families. Most families are going to have disagreements at some point in time. However, some parents never allow their children to witness any form of disagreement between them. These children grow up perceiving that marriage and family relations are perfect, only to discover the hard way that there are, indeed, times of conflict. Because of the "so-called perfect environment," the adult child now has no coping skills to handle conflicts.

I can personally vouch for the fact that I perceived several losses in my childhood erroneously. It wasn't until years later when I begin to grow in wisdom that I was able to see that I had, indeed, perceived some things based on my distorted view as a child. Truth at last brought me to a place of freedom.

"Wrong perceptions" <u>cannot always</u> be detected in children. However, as adults, we must make a conscientious effort to be on the look-out for questions the child might have in order to help him grow into adulthood free of distorted truths surrounding his loss.

Chapter 4

Building Self-Esteem

I once looked at myself in the mirror and said, "I have no idea who I am." Sure, I knew my name, but that was all I knew about me. I did not see someone in the mirror who was special and valuable, nor did I like my appearance. Would you believe that at the time of my confession in the mirror I was forty years old? It's safe to say that I had a very low self-esteem.

The search to reclaim my identity and self-esteem took me down a path that led me back to my early childhood, a place where my basic beliefs and attitudes, both positive and negative, had been established. It was the **negative** beliefs and attitudes that were established that I, like most kids, used to determine my self-esteem.

Some of the most common ways that trigger negative beliefs and attitudes in a child resulting in his self-esteem to spiral downward are:

1. being bullied by another child
2. a degrading remark by a teacher
3. making a move and not making friends right away
4. parents' divorce
5. death of a loved one
6. being made fun of because of a disability
7. low grades in school
8. not approving of his appearance
9. not receiving encouragement from adults in his life
10. not given opportunities to make some decisions on his own
11. verbal, physical, and sexual abuse

What is this thing called "**Self-Esteem**" and why is it so important? Self-Esteem can be defined as:[1]

How you feel about yourself
The opinion you have of yourself
How much value you place on yourself

Our mission as caring adults is to help a child live his life esteeming himself. This is not teaching him to brag on himself, nor is it teaching him that he will never make a mistake. Having self-esteem helps him build confidence in himself in order to achieve all the many wonderful things God has created him to be.

Self-esteem also gives him courage to try new things, as well as to go forward when he makes a mistake instead of slumping into a feeling of failure. Knowing who he really is and how valuable he is, allows him to have respect for himself, even when others say demeaning things about him. When faced with peer pressure, as most kids are, self-esteem will enable him to make wise decisions and good choices even when his friends are trying to pressure him into doing something he knows is wrong or dangerous.

I personally believe that helping a child grieve through losses in his life, while instilling in him at an early age a good sense of self-esteem, are two of the most important factors in his emotional and spiritual development. I also believe the #1 criteria for building self-esteem begins with giving him a picture through the scriptures how much God loves and values him.

I stand in awesome wonder that the same God who created heaven and earth also created all of us. Just as we view the splendor of His creation around us, I believe that He wants us to view ourselves in that manner. Why not instill this in children at a young age, especially in a day when they have so many conflicting experiences that could damage their self-worth for years to come.

To aid you in pursuing this mission as you travel this ***Journey of Healing*** with children, Bubby the Rabbit is introduced to the child in chapter 1 of the children's workbook. He will be inserting scriptures and tips in the activity section of each chapter in the children's workbook. Encourage children in these tips and scriptures daily.

Chapter 5

Answering Questions About Specific Losses

When a child experiences a loss or knows of someone who has, questions may arise out of his struggle to understand the concept of what is happening. You may be stumped about how to respond to his questions.

This chapter lists questions that our Journey Friends in the children's workbook asked on their journey, as well as common questions that other children might have on these same losses. Those losses are: **Death, Bullying, Moving, Loss of a Pet,** and **Divorce**.

Noticeably absent from the above list of losses that will be discussed in this section are physical and sexual abuse, as well as exposure to pornography. These losses must be dealt with on an individual basis, which would include the help of a professional as well as legal representation.

Remember the following 3 points when answering his questions:

1. First of all, the answers to the questions in this section have been provided for you, but they serve only as a guide to consider as you attempt to answer his questions.

2. It is best to always be honest rather than *"sugar-coating"* the answers in an effort to shield and protect him. The more clearly and honestly you answer his questions, the faster he will move forward in adapting to his loss.

3. If you do not know the answer to any additional questions he might have, it is okay to say to him: **"I don't know,"** rather than giving him a made-up answer which may not be accurate, only adding to confusion.

Death

Let's be honest -- even <u>adults</u> have many questions about death. We want to know why some people die young, while others live to be old; why some people get sick and don't get well; why accidents happen; why bad things happen to good people. If we have questions, can you imagine the curiosity and confusion children might have about death?

The Bible says in 1 Corinthians 13:12: "For now, we see through a glass darkly; but then face to face; now I know in part." (KJV) The word **"NOW"** in this verse means at the present time we are living here on this earth. Just like looking through a dark and dirty mirror, we can't see everything clearly, we won't know everything there is to know about death **NOW** in our present life.

However, we do have a responsibility as caring adults to be open and honest to answer questions we do know about death, rather than making it a taboo subject. It helps the child feel comfortable in expressing his sadness.

1. **Why do people die?**

   <u>All living things must die</u>. The Bible says in Ecclesiastes 3:2: "there is a time to be born and a time to die." (KJV) That means all living things must die, which would include people of all different ages and also animals, bugs, fish, and trees.

2. **What causes death?**

   - **Old Age** -- Most of the time people live way out into their eighties or even longer. Slowly, over the course of many years, important parts of their bodies, such as the heart, lungs, or brain wear out. When important parts of the body wear out and stops working, the person dies. Therefore, it could be said that they died of Old Age.

   - **Sickness** -- Sometimes people get sick, and the doctors cannot make them well. When this happens, their bodies stop working, and they die. But, not all people who get sick and go to the hospital die, because every day doctors discover more ways to treat sick people and make them well again.

   - **Accidents** -- Other times death happens because of accidents that cannot be prevented. The body was hurt so badly in the accident, it stopped working, and the person died.

   - **Murder** -- Murder occurs when someone deliberately kills another person.

   - **Suicide** -- Suicide occurs when a person takes his/her own life.

   - **Miscarriage** -- Sometimes babies are too weak to grow and develop in their mother's body. In that case, the mother's pregnancy ends before the baby can be born. This can still feel like a death because the family members are looking forward to a new baby in the home, and now it won't happen.

3. **Where do people go after they die?**

   God made us with a mind, body, and spirit. The Bible says in 11 Corinthians 5:8: "To be absent from the body (as in death) is to be present with the Lord." (KJV) From this verse, most Christians believe their spirit goes to heaven to be with Jesus when they die, and their bodies remain in the grave.

4. **What about me? When am I going to die?**

When a child loses a loved one, it is only natural for him to start thinking about and possibly even being fearful that he will die. That's okay, as long as he doesn't become obsessed with dying. It's also natural for him to be fearful that someone else in his family might soon die. Although children should be taught that death is a reality for all of us some day, it is important to stress to the child that he should not spend time worrying about death. Let him know that there are so many wonderful things for him to experience in life. So, instead of living in fear of dying himself, or worrying about someone close to him dying, encourage him to: *"Live his life to the fullest."*(1)

5. **I did not always obey my Dad. Was it my fault he died?**

You might hear a child saying such things as: *"If only I had prayed more, Dad would still be living,"* or I had had obeyed him, he would have lived." Stress to the child that death is **not his fault**. There was nothing he did or didn't do that could have caused the death.

6. **Since my Dad died, is it now my responsibility to take care of my mom?**

Adults are not a child's responsibility. Adults should make sure that a child's concentration is on coping with the death of a loved one for his own health. The hurt he is having won't go away unless he is given the opportunity to grieve. So, his first responsibility is to himself.

However, it is well to note that, in death, the remaining parent is also going through their own time of grief. While it should definitely be stressed to the child that he is not to "take on the burden of adult responsibilities," it is an excellent time to encourage him to do chores around the house that might be of help to his parent who is also hurting.

7. **Sometimes I hear adults say when someone dies that they are just <u>sleeping</u>. When will they wake up?**

In an effort to take away sadness from a child who is experiencing the death of a loved one, adults sometimes use phrases such as: "He is sleeping," or "He is away." This confuses a child and leads him to believe the person who died will be coming back. It is best to be honest. Let him know very gently that death is permanent and cannot be reversed. Life can't be turned back to the way it was.

8. **I heard someone say that it was God's will and a part of his plan for my mom to die. Why would God take her from me?**

Unfortunately, adults can misstate God's role in death and confuse the child rather than bring comfort. Think about it: "Do we really want children to think that it was God's idea for a drunken driver to run head on into the path of a young mother?" What kind of a picture does that paint of God? It is best to emphasize God's love that wants to help bring comfort to a child during the loss of a loved one. Love is a universal language that even the youngest of children understand. Our job as caring adults is to help children have a healthy time of grieving, not one of confusion.

9. What should I say to my friends at school?

Death can be an awkward time for a child who has experienced the death of a loved one, as well as his friends at school. Often times, the child feels as though his friends are avoiding him, leaving him to feel alone during a time when ne needs friends the most. The truth of the matter is, his friends are not avoiding him deliberately; they just don't know what to say. This is where a family member or teacher can help. Before he faces his friends, help him come up with a plan he can use to help "break the ice." It might be up to him to help his friends out of an uncomfortable position.

10. What is a funeral?

A funeral is a special ceremony which helps family and friends pay honor to the person who died. There probably will be music played at the funeral, special words said about the person who died, and a minister might give a message from the Bible. It is an opportunity to show our love for the one who died.

11. What is meant by visitation or a wake?

Visitation, or "wake" as it is sometimes called, is held the day before the funeral, or shortly before the funeral begins. It serves two purposes: (1) it is a time to honor the deceased person, and often times it is the final viewing of his body. (2) The other purpose is to give respect to the family of the person who died. It helps the family have their friends and family comfort them during this sad time in their lives.

Bullying

I'd like to begin this chapter on a personal basis. My own daughter was punched quite often at the age of 4 by a neighbor's child. Not wanting to make waves, I did not discuss it with the parents; I just tried to keep her safe when she was playing with him. She was also called rude names by "so-called friends" when she was a teenager, which I encouraged her to just ignore. When she reached adulthood, she confessed to me that the names she was called from her close friends still haunted her. How I wish I would have recognized both of these cases as a sign of bullying and put a stop to it.

My daughter's story of being bullied and the way I handled it is not uncommon. Many adults are not hearing a child's cry for help. **When their voices are not heard, a message is being sent to lonely frustrated kids that they might as well suffer in "_silence_" because no one is taking notice.**

Why are adults not hearing children's cry for help?

1. One reason a child's voice is not being heard is that bullying is frequently misunderstood by adults as a part of growing up. ***"Kids will be kids,"*** is the common thinking. Certain forms of "_teasing,_" or playing "_tag_" with someone in a playful way **is** a part of growing up and having fun. But, when things are done to another person to hurt, harm, embarrass, humiliate, and make their life miserable, it is <u>not</u> a part of growing up. Everyone has the right to feel safe and be respected.

2. Another reason kids' voices are not being heard is adults **are not aware of what bullying really is**, and assumes bullying is not happening in their community. Sadly, most of the time, it is. Bullying occurs <u>anywhere</u> in the community wherever children and youth gather.

The U.S. Department of Human Resources has initiated STOP BULLYING campaigns for years in an effort to get adults involved in their neighborhood and schools. Even with this agency's help, as well as many other anti-bullying organizations, bullying has increased to a higher level, often resulting in suicides. In 2011, President Obama held a White House Conference on bullying and stated that torment and intimidation must not be tolerated.

When adults become involved, not only is it a way to hear a child's cry for help, it's also a way to encourage other kids not being bullied to get involved with them. Most of the time kids know when bullying is going on even if they are not the one being bullied. But, for whatever reason, they sometimes choose to ignore it and become a bystander. They should be encouraged to become a part of taking a stand to stop bullying without fear of being labeled tattling.

Another good reason for adults to become involved is to **<u>help the bully</u>**. After all, they are kids who, perhaps, are crying out for help also. With proper teaching, kids who are bullies can learn to change their behavior. If left to them selves, it is possible bullying will continue even into their adult life.

This chapter is devoted to increasing adults' awareness of bullying, and to weed out misconceptions that have been formed out of ignorance to what the term "bully" means. For starters, the first misconception is this: ***A bully is not necessarily the biggest kid on the school ground. Bullies come in all shapes and sizes, and can be boys or girls.***

1. What is meant by bullying?

Bullying happens when someone repeatedly hurts, scares, or is mean to another person on purpose, and the person being bullied has a hard time defending himself.[1]

2. How can bullying be recognized? Bullying occurs in four different ways:[2]

(1) Physical Bullying -- Physical bullying hurts the body. It includes:

- hitting, punching, pushing, kicking, shoving, and choking
- getting certain people to "gang up" or "beat up" on others
- hair-pulling, biting, scratching, and pinching
- tripping and making someone fall

(2) Verbal Bullying -- Verbal bullying is talking about or to someone in a hurtful way.

- gossiping and spreading bad rumors about people
- teasing people in a mean way
- name-calling such as: "fatty," "four-eyes," "stupid," "jerk," "skinny"
- scaring someone over and over again on purpose
- making fun of people with a disability or not including them in activities
- blaming and accusing someone for things they didn't do

(3) Emotional Bullying -- Emotional bullying plays on the mind and hurts inside.

- leaving someone out of group activities on purpose
- ignoring someone or giving them the "silent treatment"
- making faces or bad gestures with your hands at someone
- giving mean, dirty, or threatening looks
- making fun of someone of a different race or religion

(4) Cyber Bullying -- Cyber bullying is hurting someone through the use of technology.

- writing rude blogs on the internet
- sending nasty emails
- talking about someone in a chat room
- text messaging rude comments
- yahoo instant messaging
- web pages

3. Why do kids say and do mean things to others?

Everyone has different life experiences, which may lead a child into bullying others. As sad as these situations may be, it is still no excuse for bullying. Everyone can choose to act in better ways, regardless of his circumstances. Nonetheless, understanding "why" kids say and do mean things to others might help adults have compassion on the one doing the bulling in order to help him change his behavior. Remember, we are talking about kids, and all kids need our help in order for them to grow into responsible adults.

(1) Unfortunately, kids sometimes bully others as a result of their **home environment**.

- Some parents do not teach their children about being kind to others.
- Parents who allow their child to watch violence in movies, TV, or video games run the risk of their child acting out in destructive behavior toward others.

- If a child has watched his parents or other family members get their way by pushing, yelling, and shouting, he often will model their behavior.
- Some children haven't been taught how to express his feelings or given the opportunity to express his feelings; therefore, he has no knowledge how to control his anger.

(2) Often times a child will resort to bullying as a means of getting **attention**. His thinking is that if he is not getting the attention he longs for at home, or even at school and other places where children gather, he will demand it by bullying.

(3) **Feelings of insecurity** usually bring about a negative response in all of us. To a child, bullying can become a means of making him look tough to compensate for insecure feelings.

(4) **He may have been bullied himself**, and is using bullying innocent people as a payback for what has happened to him.(3)

(5) Some researchers say many bullies actually have a high self-esteem, but they bully because **they are aggressive, hot-tempered, easily-angered, impulsive, have a low tolerance for frustration, and have need to dominate others**.(4)

(6) Kids who cyber bully often do so because they **think it is funny** when they can hide behind a computer screen and frighten someone else.

How to Stop Bullying

When it comes to stopping bullying among children, we each have a role to play, which includes: parents, students, schools, churches, and even those who have been victims of being bullied as a child. In essence, it is a community project.

The following is a few basic ways to instill in children how to stop bullying, as well as pointers to prevent it from occurring.

1. **Do not fight back**

   It is not a good idea to fight back, particularly if the child is being bullied physically. Fighting back could cause someone to get hurt badly. Besides, it won't solve the bully's problem; he/she would only continue. A bully gets satisfaction out of seeing others upset.

2. **Tell an adult when being bullied**

   While a child should not fight back, neither should he ignore what the bully is doing to him or someone else either. Ignoring a bully will not stop him from bullying; it gives him the idea it is okay to continue. *"**Telling is not tattling**."* Kids do not like to be called *"Tattle Tells."* Teach them that telling is a means of staying safe.

3. **Avoid unsupervised areas**, such as school bathroom, locker room, or dark halls at any facility.

4. **Never walk anywhere alone** -- Play it safe by walking with a friend or more preferably with a group.

5. Act Confident

While there is never an excuse for being bullied, being more confident will keep a child from being an easy target. Encourage him to participate in activities which will help build self-confidence such as: sports, dancing, scouts, or music. Not only will these activities help him build confidence, but also will help him develop new friends. [See Chapter 4 – Building Self-Esteem]

6. Safeguards to prevent cyber-bullying

- Do not give out personal information online or in conversation
- Do not tell anyone, not even friends, your passwords
- If someone sends a mean or threatening message, do not answer it. Save it and show it to a trusted adult

7. Do nice things for others

Bullying is not just about doing mean things; it's also about encouraging children to do nice things for other kids. For example: Encourage him to sit with a child who is sitting alone at lunch; do not ignore people as though they are invisible.

8. Be a Good Samaritan and Help Stop Bullying

Jesus told the story of a man who was traveling from Jerusalem to Jericho when he was attacked by robbers. They beat him, took his money, stripped him of his clothes, and left him beside the road to die. (Luke 10:37 TLB)

The first person who came by, saw the man lying there, crossed over to the other side of the road, and continued on his way. A little while later, another person came along, saw the man lying there, but also left him lying there.

Finally, a third man came along. When he saw the man lying there, he stopped and help him. He put medicine on the wounds and wrapped them with bandages. That isn't all he did. He took the man to an inn so he could get some rest. He gave the innkeeper some money and told him to take care of the man. "Give him anything he needs."

Jesus ended the story by saying: **"Now, you go and do the same for someone."**

Moving

It is a scary thing for a child when he has to suddenly leave his best friend, give up his position on the soccer team, be the new kid in class, or ride the school bus with 25 new kids. When a move is taking place because of a death in the family or divorce, it brings with it added stress for the entire family.

My family made a move to another state when my two daughters were 11 and 15 due to a job transfer. Because they seemed to adapt socially, I was not aware that the move had such an impact on them until years later.

Regardless of the circumstances of a move, children need a caring adult to answer all their questions about the move, as well as help them make the transition from one location to another, whether it is out of state or locally.

1. **Why do I have to move?**

The answer to this question will vary according to the family's circumstances. Job transfers, divorce, death of a spouse, or finances -- all play a role in why a family makes a move. Whatever the reason for the move, try to explain as simply as you can why the move must occur. He may not fully understand the reason for it, but at least you are letting him know all his questions about the move are important. Reassure him you are available to answer any further questions he might have in the days to come.

2. **What does the new place look like?**

If at all possible, allow him to go with you to check out his new place before the move. This will help him begin to feel a little more secure, as well as possibly get him excited about a new place. If you are moving far away and it's not possible to visit the new place prior to the move, there are other ways to help him become familiar with his new home, such as: check out books from the library, write the Chamber of Commerce, or do an internet search for information about his new city and state to share with him.

3. **Will I be able to take my dog?**

This question must be answered according to your circumstances. For example: (1) If you are moving into an apartment complex, certain complexes will not allow pets. (2) If you are moving in with relatives during a divorce proceeding, the relative might prefer not to have a pet at their home. If the pet is not allowed to make the move with the family, assure the child you will find a loving home for his pet. Discuss options with him so that he feels comfortable with the place and people where his pet will be living.

4. **Will I be able to take all my toys?**

Most of us are collectors by nature, including kids. Moving can be a time to get rid of excess baggage. However, with kids, it has to be done very gently. Remember that the move itself is a loss to him. Losing "his things" that are special to him could make the move even harder. A good rule of thumb to discuss with him is separating the toys, books, and clothes into three piles, such as the following: (1)

- things he'd like to keep
- things he doesn't want and could be given away to other kids
- things which are worn out and can be thrown away

5. Will I get to see my friends again?

First of all, if the family is moving out of state, do not give him false hope by saying, "we will visit your friends when school is out." That is not always feasible because of the distance involved. However, make sure the child realizes that his present friends will always have a special place in his heart. Also, reassure him that he will make new friends. They will not replace the friends he is leaving, but he will make friends and start making another memory as he did with his old friends.

Note: It should be pointed out that the child's friends who are left behind after a friend moves, are also going through a loss of their own. They are losing a special friend with whom they have shared many fun times. Please do not overlook these children. They, too, need help in working through the loss of their friend.

6. How can I say goodbye to my friends?

Saying goodbye is never easy, but it can be made into a fun time in the days prior to moving. One month prior to moving with our two daughters, our house literally turned into "the local swimming pool," as one swimming party after another became the norm. Other ways you might want to consider for the child to say goodbye are:

(1) Have a party for all his friends. While the friends are at the party, get their telephone number, address, and email address for him to take with him to his new residence.

(2) Give him an opportunity to pay a visit to other people who have made a positive influence in his life such as a favorite teacher, pastor, or neighbor down the street.

(3) Take pictures of rooms in your house where birthday parties and holidays were celebrated to keep as a memory. Also take pictures of the outside of the house. I had an artist paint a picture of former houses my family has lived in, and they hang in our current home. It is a wonderful reminder of memories in a former house.

(4) Set aside a day to visit and take pictures of some of his favorite places in town such as the park, skating rink, or favorite ice cream store.

7. Use the move as an opportunity to teach a lesson in faith with the story of Abraham.

Can you imagine not only moving from your neighborhood, but moving to another country? That's exactly what God called Abraham to do a very long time ago. God told Abraham, "Leave your own country behind you, and your own people, and go to the land I will guide you to." (Genesis 12:1 – TLB)

Picture in your mind the following scene:

- There were no cameras to take pictures of the friends he was leaving behind.
- There were no telephones to call his friends once he was in another country.
- There was no postal service to mail them a letter.
- There was no internet service to send them an email.

Can you imagine what your life would be like if you were faced with a move like Abraham and had no way to stay in touch with your friends? Even though Abraham did not have all the conveniences we have today to help him adjust to his new move, he had a very special tool in his life to help him adjust to the new changes brought on by the move. **That tool was faith in God**.

> "Faith is the confident assurance that something we want is going to happen. It is the certainty that what we hope for is waiting for us, even though we cannot see it up ahead." (Hebrews 11:1 TLB)

Abraham's faith in God helped him trust God to take care of him in his new country, no matter what lay ahead of him. **Why not memorize Hebrews 11:1 and let your faith in God work during your move the same way it worked for Abraham.**

Losing a Pet

The most obvious way of losing a pet is death. However, sometimes a pet runs away from home and cannot find its way back home. Another way of losing a pet is because of a move. Some apartments, as well as subdivisions, do not allow pets. No matter which way a child experiences the loss of a pet, it hurts and he is going to need help in answering his questions and making adjustments to his loss.

1. **What causes an animal to die?**

   When an animal dies, his body is no longer working. The heart stops beating, and the body no longer needs to eat or sleep. Possible reasons for his death are:

   - **Old Age** -- Most of the time animals live a very long time. Slowly, over the course of many years, their body wears out just like a toy that is old and breaks apart. When important parts of the body, such as the heart and lungs stop working, the animal dies.

   - **Accidents** -- Sometimes death happens because of accidents which cannot be prevented, such as being run over by a car. The body was hurt so badly in the accident, it's heart stopped working and the animal died.

   - **Sickness** -- Sometimes animals get sick. If an animal is in a lot of pain and the veterinarian knows he will not get better, the parents and the vet sometimes decide the animal should be allowed to die to ease his pain. In order to do this, the vet will give him a shot of medicine which helps him die peacefully. Deciding to help a pet die is a hard thing to do. Stress to the child this decision was made because his parents and the vet did not want to see his pet in pain.

2. **My mom said my pet ran away. How long will it be before he returns?**

   Some animals do run away. However, do not use that as a reason for the death of an animal or the reason an animal cannot be included in a move the family is making. *"He ran away,"* makes the child think his pet will be coming home.

3. **My dad said he would buy me another pet, but I don't want a replacement.**

   Losses of any nature cannot be replaced. However, the decision to quickly obtain a new pet may vary for each family. For some families, adopting a new pet quickly is the right thing to do, but for others it is not because the child needs time to grieve the emotional loss of his pet. In either case, there are some important lessons that can be learned.

   (1) Make sure the child knows that no other animal can take his pet's place, and that the family will always cherish the memory of the special pet he had in his life.

   (2) Stress to him he has a lot of love to give another animal that needs a good home.

4. **Do animals go to heaven?**

   The Bible does not give any clear direction. You might say it is silent on the subject. However, in the absence of any clear direction in the Bible, we must always realize God is love. In fact, Psalm 36:5-6 talks about His love for animals: "Your steadfast love, O Lord, is as great as all the heavens. Your faithfulness reaches beyond the clouds. Your justice is as solid as God's mountains. Your decisions are full of wisdom as the oceans are with water. You are concerned for men and animals alike." (TLB)

5. Use the loss of the child's pet as an opportunity to teach a lesson in trust and how much God loves all of His creation with the story of Noah and the Ark.

The Bible tells a story showing us just how much God loves animals. It is the story of Noah and the Ark. (Genesis 6-8)

The people in Noah's day were very wicked, so God decided to send a flood that would destroy all the people on the earth, except Noah and his family who were very good people.

To spare Noah and his family, God told Noah to build an ark to live in when it came time for the flood to begin. He also gave Noah instructions to take two of every kind of animal in the ark with him so they wouldn't drown either.

When it came time for the flood to sweep over the face of the earth, Noah and his family and the animals entered the ark. Can you imagine living in the ark for forty days and nights with elephants, tigers, lions, dogs, cats, bugs, rabbits, frogs, and giraffes?

The Good News is: When the flood was over, Noah and his family and all the animals marched off the ark alive.

**If God took care of all those animals during the flood,
trust Him to take care of your pet also, even after his death.**

Divorce

Probably the #1 question most children ask when their parents tell them the news of an impending divorce is "Why?" They feel as though their world is falling apart when told that the two people they love the most in the world will no longer be living under the same roof. "Why are you doing this, I don't understand," they cry out.

Most of the time, the real reason for parents divorcing are bigger than kids can really understand. Wise parents and caring adults working with children whose parents are about to divorce or have already divorced should never attempt to explain the problems in a relationship between a man and woman. Remember it is a time to help the child transition and heal from his loss, not a time to place blame and especially not a time to talk about relationship issues that a child wouldn't understand anyway.

Simply put, the "why" question could be best answered by saying: "When we married, we really loved one another and made a vow to stay together forever. However, we are having arguments that we can't solve, so we feel it is best to divorce."

While that answer may not completely satisfy him, it does let him know that you care about all his concerns and questions. After all, his world is about to change in a big way, and he is entitled to know the answers as best as you can give him at this time.

The following are some of the most common questions children ask.

1. **What does *"divorce"* mean?**

Divorce means parents have decided they will no longer stay married to each other and will live in separate homes.

2. **Is the divorce my fault?**

The divorce is absolutely not the fault of the child! A child might think his misbehaving, having a dirty room, or bad grades caused the divorce. Divorce is about parents having problems with each other, not problems with their kids. Try this example as a means of reassuring him. "If two of your neighborhood friends got into a fight while you were sitting at home watching TV, did you cause the fight?" Absolutely not; likewise, there is nothing you did or didn't do that caused the breakup. No one can make two people divorce. The two people decide those things for themselves.

3. **If the divorce is not my fault, whose fault is it, Mom or Dad's?**

It is important to remember: <u>divorce is about change, not blame.</u>[1] The change in a family is not about who is right or wrong or who is good or bad. Usually parents try their best to resolve their problems, but for whatever reasons, they couldn't. Instead of worrying about who is to blame, encourage the child to think about how he can adjust to a new chapter in his life.

4. **Is the divorce forever?**

It is normal for children to hope that their parents get back together, but it only happens in rare cases that parents will get back together again.[2] Be honest with the child and try not to build false hope, but instead, help him find a way to be happy and healthy, even though his parents are divorced.

5. **Who is going to take care of me?**

Children need to feel secure. When they see their parents splitting up, "who is going to take care of me" is a big concern. Reassure them that no matter who they may be living with -- Mom, Dad, or Grandparents -- they will be taken care of as they have always been. This might also be a good time to discuss visitation rights. If for some reason, one parent is not allowed to have visitation rights, that needs to be discussed gently also.

6. **If my parents stopped loving one another, does that mean they will stop loving me?**

This question is a big one that needs careful explanation and encouragement to the child. Say to him over and over again: "Your parents will never stop loving you." "You are very special to both of them." "They divorced each other, not you."

To help him understand love, it might help to explain to him that love has many faces, and they all look different such as:

- the love between a child and grandparents
- the love between two friends
- the love between man and woman
- the love between parents and their child

7. **What are the changes that will take place after a divorce?**

Changes will vary in each family. Some of the changes that might take place are:

(1) He might have to move to another house, and even move away from close friends or relatives. Since he will have 2 homes, he will probably spend part of the time with one parent and part of the time with the other.

(2) There is a possibility the family will have less money, which means he might have a change in how much is spent on him for clothes and activities. Reassure him that his basic needs will be met and that he will not lack for anything.

(3) Holidays will change. His time will likely be divided between people in two houses.

(4) He might not be able to see both sets of grandparents as often as he once did if he has to make a move away from them.

8. **What can I do to fix it?**

Sometimes children think if they are extra nice to their parents, or work harder at being a good kid they can fix their parents' problems. Some children resort to acting really bad in the hope their parents stay together to take care of them. Make sure the child realizes he can do nothing to fix his parents' problems. The problems his parents are having are not about him; the problem is with each other and he cannot fix it.

9. **What can I tell my friends?**

Children often feel embarrassed or ashamed in front of their friends when their parents divorce. Help them be prepared to face their friends who ask questions about the divorce by saying something along these lines: "We are still a family; we just don't live together anymore."

10. Do I still have a family?

When there is a divorce and the family goes their separate ways, kids sometimes wonder about whether they are still called a family or not. Actually, most kids would probably define family as "a mom and dad and their kids who all live in the same house together."

The truth is, that is what God intended when He created man and woman. The Bible says, *"God created man and woman in his own image and told them to be fruitful, multiply, and replenish the earth."* [Genesis 1:28 KJV] Unfortunately, it doesn't always happen that way.

Does that mean the child doesn't have a family after a divorce? Absolutely not! What it means is that we must help re-define the meaning of family for him. Think about this definition of family:

Family means people who provide
love, support, advice, comfort, time, and friendship to each other.

With that definition in mind, have him think of the people who have given those things to him. No doubt, he will name such people as: grandparents, close friends, cousins, aunts, uncles, school teachers, or a pastor.

Stress to him that with all these wonderful people in his life, along with his mom and dad, even though he doesn't live in the same house with both of them, he still has a family.

Epilogue

Dear Caring Adult:

Thank you for joining us on our journey. You have been an instrument God has used to help change a child's life forever as you traveled with him on his ***Journey of Healing***. For that, I'm sure God is smiling down upon you from heaven. Our children deserve to grow up without excess baggage from their childhood. Unfortunately, because losses are a normal part of life, we can't always protect children from having losses in their lives, but we can help them cope with each loss.

So, hats off to you for, not only giving of your time, but for the comfort and compassion you have shown the child you walked with on his/her ***Journey of Healing***. Also, a big hats off to educators and children's ministers who have chosen to use this workbook in a group setting to familiarize children with the concepts of grieving. Hopefully, it will build a foundation in them at an early age which will carry into their adult lives as they are faced with losses.

One final reminder: ***"Healing is a process."*** With that thought in mind, a child may need to revisit some of the steps in the workbook to help cope with the pain of his loss, particularly around holidays and birthdays. Those days were fond memories in a child's life of special days, and now their loss is preventing them from sharing that special day with someone they love. Therefore, revisit with him the steps which are applicable to his needs.

May God bless and continue to use you to comfort and guide children through losses in their young lives.

Sincerely,

Martha Bush

Notes

Introduction

1. Wright H. Norman, (1997). <u>Recovering From the Losses in Life</u>. Fleming H. Revell. pg. 10.

Chapter 1: Supporting a Grieving Child

1. <u>www.childrensgrief.net</u>. *"Helping the Grieving Child in School.,* Linda Goldman.
2. Ibid.
3. The Dougy Center, (2004). <u>35 Ways to Help a Grieving Child</u>. pg. 13.
4. Wright, H. Norman, (2004). <u>It's Okay to Cry</u>. Water Brook Press. Pgs. 66-73.
5. Ibid.

Chapter 2: Understanding Feelings

1. Minirth, Frank, and Meir Paul, (1994). <u>Happiness is a Choice</u>. Baker Books. Pg. 71.
2. Ibid.
3. <u>www.nationalmentalhealthassociation.org</u> *"Depression in Children."*

Chapter 3: Recognizing Perception

1. Guralnik, David B., Editor in Chief, (1982), <u>Webster's New World Dictionary</u>. Simon and Schuster, pg. 336.

Chapter 4: Building Self-Esteem

1. <u>www.kidshealth.com</u>

Chapter 5: Answering Questions About Specific Losses

Death

1. Kids Health, *"When Somebody Dies."*
<u>www.kidshealth.org</u>

Bullying

1. United States Department of Health and Human Services, *"Stop Bullying Now!"*
<u>www.hrsa.gov</u>
2. Ibid.
3. KidsPeace, *"Bully Tips for Parents.*
<u>www.kidspeace.org</u>
4. Safe Youth, *"Bullying."*
<u>www.safeyouth.org</u>.

Moving

1. Century 21, *"Smooth Moves."*

   www.century 21.com

Loss of a Pet

1. Pet Education, *"Grief and the Loss of a Pet."*

   www.peteducation.com

Divorce

1. Internet, Woman's Divorce, *"Explaining Divorce to Children."*

   www.womansdivorce.com

2. Internet, It's My Life, *"Divorce, the Big Question."*

   www.pbskids.org/itsmylife

Bible Translations

Verses marked NIV are taken from the New International Version
Verses marked LB are taken from The Living Bible
Verses marked NLT are taken from The New Living Bible
Verses marked KJV are taken from King James Version

Resource List

Suggested Websites and Books

Websites

1. www.kidshealth.com

2. www.hospice.net

3. www.kidspeace.org

4. www.stopbullyingnow.com

5. www.centruy21.com

6. www.petplace.com

7. www.womansdivorce.com

Books

1. Wright, H. Norman: <u>Recovering From the Losses of Life</u>.

2. Wright, H. Norman: <u>It's Okay to Cry</u>

3. Goldman, Linda: <u>Life and Loss</u>: <u>A Guide to Help Grieving Children</u>

4. The Dougy Center, The National Center for Grieving Children and Families: <u>35 Ways to Help a Grieving Child</u>

About the Author

Martha Bush grew up on a farm in Donalsonville, Georgia. She graduated from Valdosta State College, Valdosta, Georgia, with a BS degree in Business Education. After graduating from college, Martha began her teaching career that spanned grades 5-12 in both public and Christian schools. She also taught adult vocational courses in the Atlanta school system.

Her love for teaching led her into areas outside the school system as she began teaching Bible study courses in jails, prisons, and at her local church. She also writes a monthly inspirational post at www.createdwoman.net and is a contributing editor for Created Woman Magazine.

In addition, Martha is a contributor to girlfriendscoffeehour.com and a member of the Orange County Christian Writers Guild.

Through her years of teaching, as well as being an avid reader of human behavior and grief counseling from noted Christian psychologists, she recognized how a team effort can help build a foundation in children at an early age that will enable them to cope with the losses in their lives. She believes this team, made of up parents, grandparents, educators, and spiritual leaders, can guide a child to healing from losses he or she might experience. They can do this simply by recognizing his pain, listening to his pain and then teaching the child how to apply the principles of God's Word to his hurting heart. This led her to write ***Helping Hurting Children: A Journey of Healing.***

Martha resides in Orange, Texas, with her husband, Glen. They are the parents of two grown daughters who have blessed them with three beautiful grandchildren.

Should you be interested in becoming a caring adult, visit www.marthafbush.com for more information on how you can purchase the books or email her at: martha@marthafbush.com